9 Months Later: Preserving Happiness

***

Postpartum Journal

2

YouAreCreators
P.O. Box 756
Tinley Park, IL 60477

hello@thestorkbag.com
info@mommymaidd.com
youarecreators2@gmail.com

ISBN-10: 0692879234

ISBN-13: 978-0692879238

First Edition

Dedication:

Justin Jr, Joshua and Jaxon. Thank you for making me a mommy.

This Journal Belongs To:

_____

The Date I Became a Mom:

_____

8

Date:_____

Date:_____

Date:_____

Date:_____

Date:_____

Date:_____

Gratitude break:

I'm grateful for:

_____

_____

_____

_____

_____

_____

_____

_____

_____

_____

_____

_____

_____

_____

_____

Date:_____

_____

_____

_____

_____

_____

_____

_____

_____

_____

_____

_____

_____

_____

_____

_____

Be Present:
Stop, and take 60 seconds to be present. Take in the smells and sounds of your surroundings, feel the air on your skin.

Date: _____

_____

_____

_____

_____

_____

_____

_____

_____

_____

_____

_____

_____

_____

_____

Date:_____

_____

_____

_____

_____

_____

_____

_____

_____

_____

_____

_____

_____

_____

_____

_____

"Where there is love there is life."
– Mohandas Gandhi

Date:_____

_____

_____

_____

_____

_____

_____

_____

_____

_____

_____

_____

_____

Date:_____

_____

_____

_____

_____

_____

_____

_____

_____

_____

_____

_____

_____

_____

_____

_____

_____

_____

_____

_____

_____

_____

_____

_____

_____

_____

_____

_____

_____

_____

_____

_____

Date:_____

_____

_____

_____

_____

_____

_____

_____

_____

_____

_____

_____

_____

_____

_____

_____

_____

_____

Date:_____

Date:_____

Date: _____

_____

_____

_____

_____

_____

_____

_____

_____

_____

_____

_____

_____

_____

_____

Date:_____

Date:_____

Date:_____

_____
_____
_____
_____
_____
_____
_____
_____
_____
_____
_____
_____
_____
_____
_____
_____
_____

Date:_____

Gratitude break:

3 People I'm grateful for:
(Doesn't have to be anyone you know personally)

_____

_____

_____

_____

_____

_____

_____

_____

Date:_____

Date:_____

_____

_____

_____

_____

_____

_____

_____

_____

_____

_____

_____

_____

_____

_____

_____

_____

Date: _____

_____

_____

_____

_____

_____

_____

_____

_____

_____

_____

_____

_____

_____

_____

_____

Date:_____

_____

_____

_____

_____

_____

_____

_____

_____

_____

_____

_____

_____

_____

_____

_____

_____

Date:_____

_____
_____
_____
_____
_____
_____
_____
_____
_____
_____
_____
_____
_____
_____
_____
_____

Date:_____

Date:_____

Date:_____

_____

_____

_____

_____

_____

_____

_____

_____

_____

_____

_____

_____

_____

_____

_____

_____

_____

_____

Date:_____

_____
_____
_____
_____
_____
_____
_____
_____
_____
_____
_____
_____
_____
_____
_____
_____

_____

_____

_____

_____

_____

_____

_____

_____

_____

_____

_____

_____

_____

_____

_____

_____

_____

Date:_____

Gratitude break:

Things I'm looking forward to:

_____

_____

_____

_____

_____

_____

_____

_____

_____

_____

_____

_____

_____

_____

_____

Date:_____

Date:_____

Date:_____

Date:_____

I tried to find the perfect mom and model her; I searched high and low to find her. 'How would she look? How would she talk? How would her kids look?' Long story short, I didn't find her, but I did find myself and I became my definition of the perfect mom with lots of imperfections.
-Ericka Perry-

Date:_____

Date:_____

_____

_____

_____

_____

_____

_____

_____

_____

_____

_____

_____

_____

_____

_____

_____

_____

Date:_____

Date:_____

_____

_____

_____

_____

_____

_____

_____

_____

_____

_____

_____

_____

_____

_____

_____

_____

Date:_____

_____

_____

_____

_____

_____

_____

_____

_____

_____

_____

_____

_____

_____

_____

_____

_____

Date:_____

Date:_____

Date:_____

Date: _____

_____
_____
_____
_____
_____
_____
_____
_____
_____
_____
_____
_____
_____
_____
_____

I had to keep reminding myself, that it was ok to make a mistake or to make someone wait and put my needs first.
-Ericka Perry-

Date:_____

Date:_____

Date:_____

Date:_____

Date:_____

Date:_____

The Beauty of Motherhood:

If I weren't a mother I wouldn't be doing this. I wouldn't have created this journal; I wouldn't have created The Stork Bag, 9 Months of Happiness, none of that. Because I am a mother, I have an inner desire to serve other mothers. I know how important it is to nurture mothers the way they nurture those around them.

What is something that you attribute to being a mother in your life?

_____

_____

_____

_____

_____

_____

_____

_____

Date:

Date:_____

Date:_____

Date:_____

Date:_____

Date:_____

Date:_____

Preserving Happiness Tip:

Where's your happy place?

My happy place is by the water. I love large bodies of water, lakes, rivers, and oceans--- I love to sit near the water and be present. I love the sound of the water and the smells that come along with it. That is my happy place. Think about what your happy place is. Maybe you have more than one, either way think about it in its entirety. How does it smell, how does it sound, how does it feel on your skin? Once you have this happy place in your mind, practice going there when you need to take a break and allow yourself to drift away to your happy place.

Date:_____

Date:_____

Date:_____

_____

_____

_____

_____

_____

_____

_____

_____

_____

_____

_____

_____

_____

_____

_____

_____

Date:_____

"I remember looking at those smooth little feet and round little toes and thinking, "I did this, I grew this perfect little being inside my body." I felt proud." –
Ericka Perry-

Date:_____

_____

_____

_____

_____

_____

_____

_____

_____

_____

_____

Date:_____

Date:_____

Date:
_____

Quiet time. You deserve

quiet time.

Date:_____

Date:_____

Date:_____

Date:_____

Date:_____

Date:_____

Date:_____

Date:_____

Date:_____

Date: _____

I Am:

The two words "I AM" are a strong declaration of expression. What you put behind these words can become powerful identifiers in how you see yourself. What are some of your I AMs?

Here are some of mine:
I Am Strong
I Am Determined
I Am a Leader

Your turn:

I Am _____

I Am _____

I Am _____

I Am _____

I Am _____

I Am _____

Date:

Date:_____

Date:_____

_____
_____
_____
_____
_____
_____
_____
_____
_____
_____
_____
_____
_____
_____
_____
_____

Date:_____

Preserving Happiness Tip:

Essential Oils are great all natural staples to have in your home. Among their many uses, certain essential oils are great mood enhancers, too. Here are a few:

Ylang Ylang Oil

Rose Oil

Lavender Oil

Chamomile Oil

Bergamot Oil

Try investing in an essential oil diffuser. Drop a few drops of your favorite oil in and create your own spa at home.

Date:_____

Date:

Date:_____

Date:_____

Date:_____

Date:_____

Date:

Motherhood Affirmations:

Affirmations are declared statements that allow you to consciously control your thoughts. Repeating affirmations can have a positive impact on the way you feel and the way you see yourself. Here are a few affirmations to help you get started.

I am a strong woman.
I am a great caregiver and nurturer.
I am important and deserve all good things that come my way.
My mind and body are my temple and I will do all I can to maintain my well-being.

I encourage you to add some additional affirmations that resonate best with you.

_____

_____

_____

_____

_____

The very damaging, frightening part of postpartum is the lack of perspective and the lack of priority and understanding what is really important.
-Brooke Shields-

Date:_____

_____

_____

_____

_____

_____

_____

_____

_____

_____

Date:_____

Date:_____

Date:_____

Date:_____

The Beauty of Motherhood:

My life has changed for the better now because:

_____

_____

_____

_____

_____

_____

_____

_____

_____

_____

_____

_____

_____

Date:_____

Date:_____

Date:_____

Date:_____

Separate Identity:

What makes __ME__ happy?

_____

_____

_____

_____

_____

_____

_____

_____

_____

_____

_____

_____

_____

Date:_____

Date:_____

Date:_____

_____

_____

_____

_____

_____

_____

_____

_____

_____

_____

_____

_____

_____

_____

_____

Date:_____

Breathe...

What is happiness anyway?

Happiness is defined as: a state of well-being
and contentment : JOY
Merriam-Webster

What is happiness to you?

_____

_____

_____

_____

_____

_____

_____

_____

_____

_____

_____

_____

_____

_____

_____

_____

_____

_____

_____

_____

_____

_____

_____

_____

_____

_____

_____

Pay it forward:

I truly hope this journal was beneficial to you. It is my hope that even if you didn't write one word in this journal, you at least got something from one of the quotes, tips or encouraging text. If you did, pay it forward. Share it with someone, anyone. You never know who may need it...

-Ericka

Made in the USA
Middletown, DE
11 May 2021